The Game Goes On

By: Monica Garrett
Illustrated By: Prabir Sarkar

Copyright © 2024 by Monica Garrett- All rights reserved.

All rights reserved. No part of this publication may be reproduced, distributed, duplicated, or transmitted in any form or by any means including photocopying, recording part of this document in either electronic means or in printed format. Recording of this publication is strictly prohibited and any storage of this document is not allowed unless with written permission from the publisher.

All rights reserved.

Respective authors own all copyrights

not held by the publisher.

Marion and his mother Ms. Myla are preparing

to go to the park to play basketball and attend the carnival.

They strap on their helmets, pack the basketball and

water bottles, and get on their bikes.

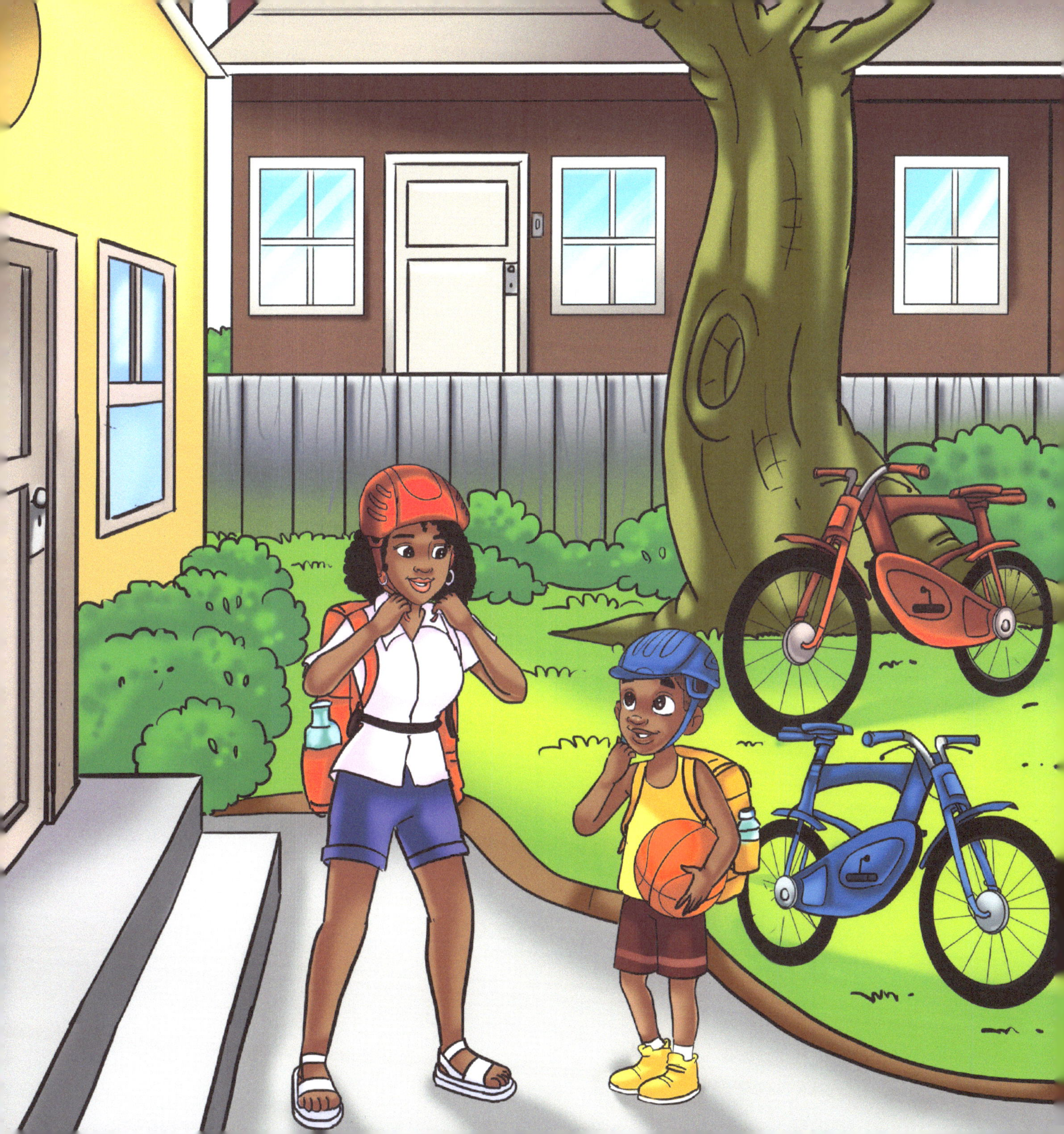

Marion's friend Layla wants to join them.

She receives permission from her dad to go with them.

Marion and Ms. Myla meet Layla

at the end of her driveway.

They ride away and head to the park,

enjoying the breeze on a nice sunny day.

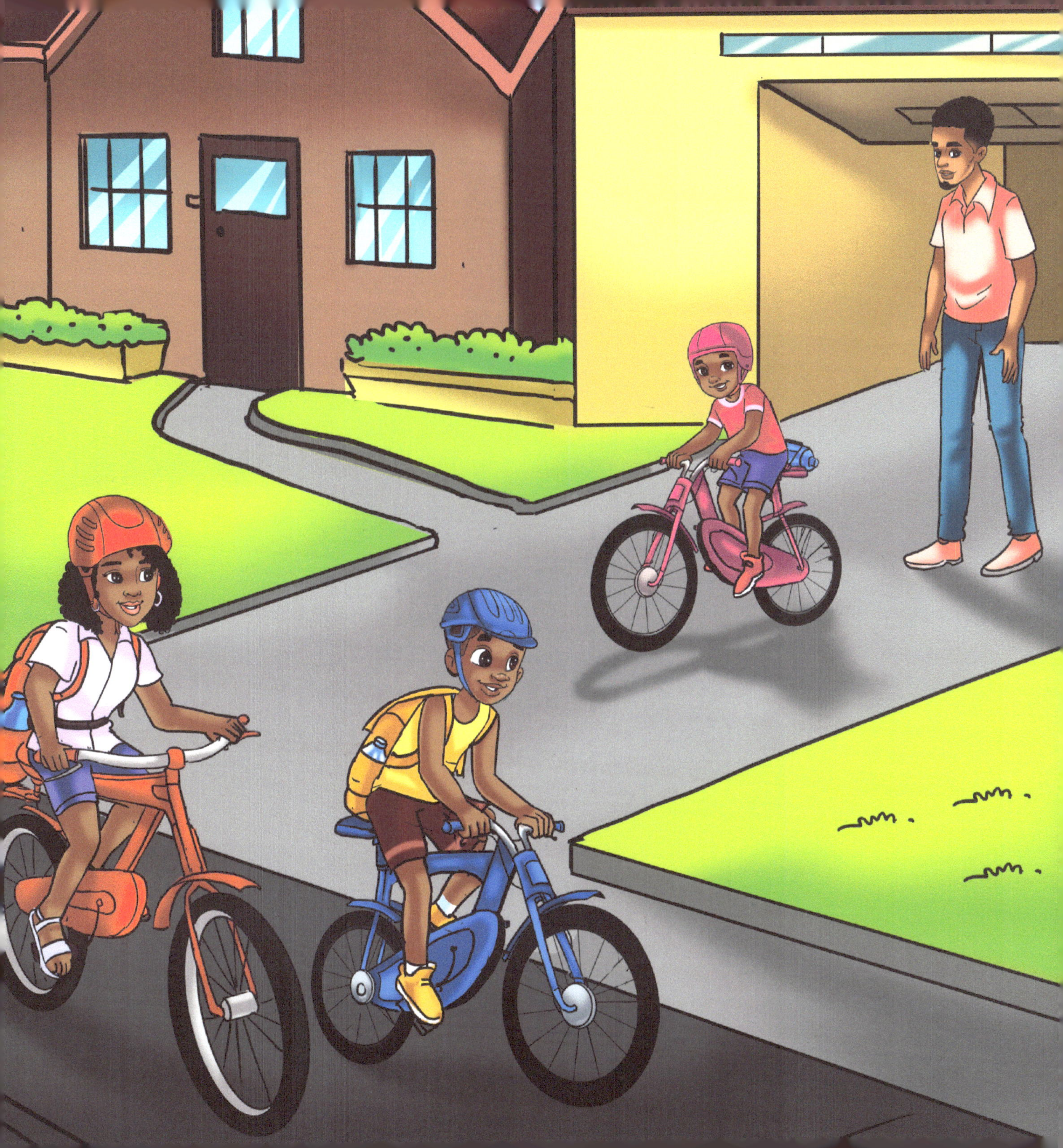

They arrive at the park and lock their bikes on the bike rack.

Checking their shoes for loose strings,

they can't wait to start their game.

Looking over at the carnival, they are amazed

at the number of people enjoying the rides.

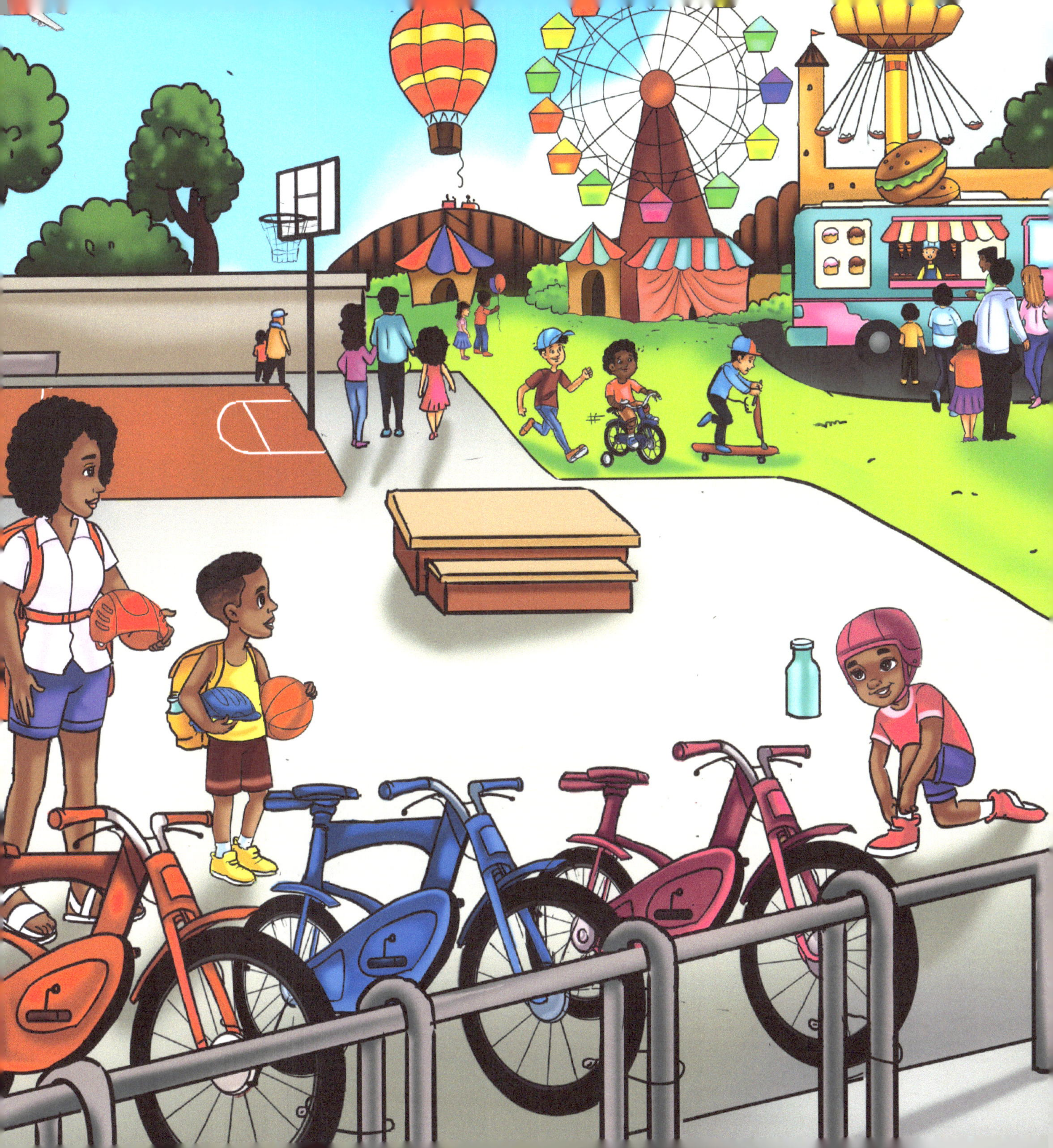

While walking to the basketball court,

Ms. Myla sat at the nearby picnic table ready

to watch their basketball game.

They take a quick drink of water,

and now it is time to play basketball.

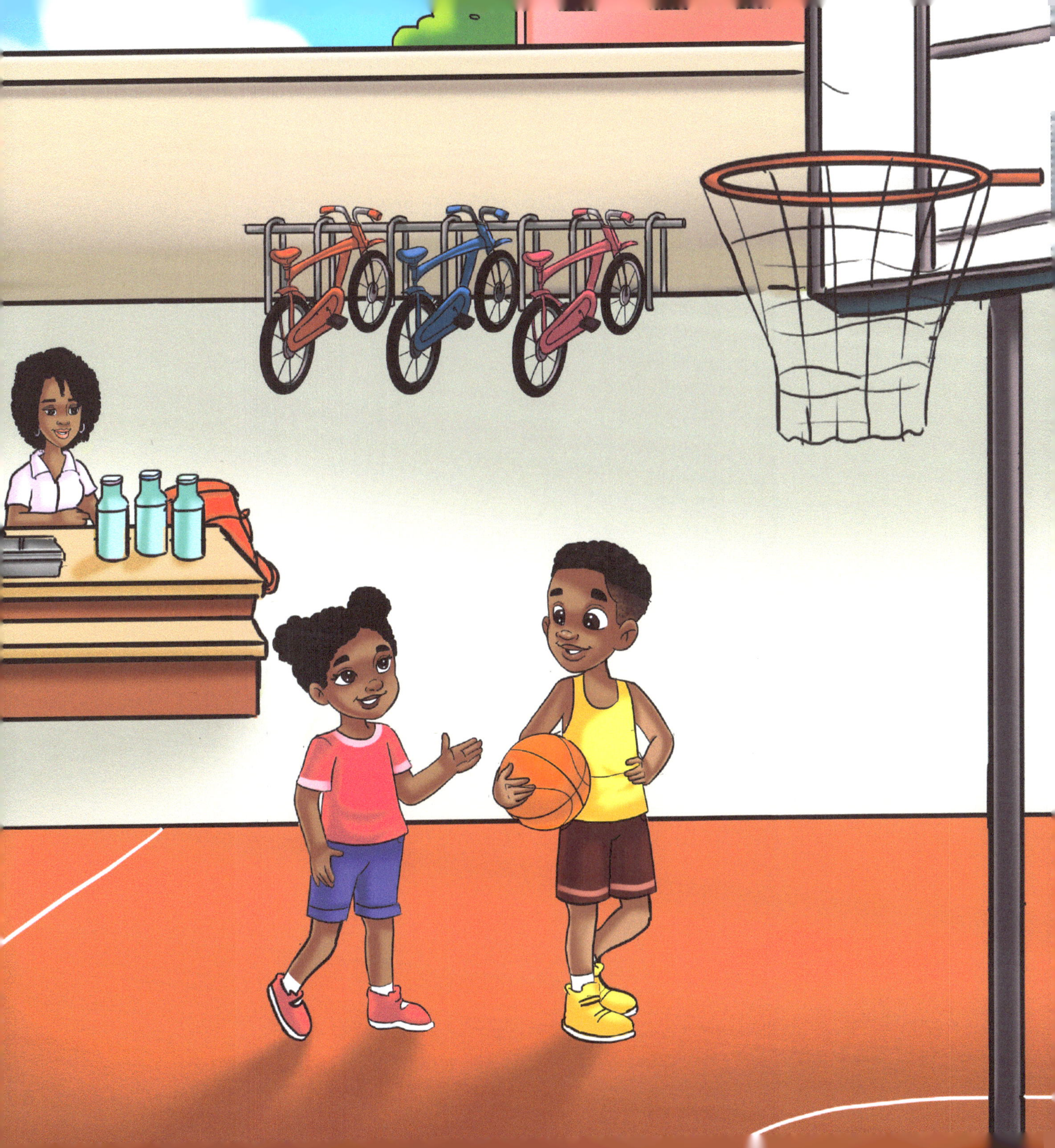

Layla has the ball first.

She dribbles down the court, creates space to shoot the ball,

and makes the first basket.

"Good shot Layla", says Marion! "Great job",

says Ms. Myla as she cheers from the sideline.

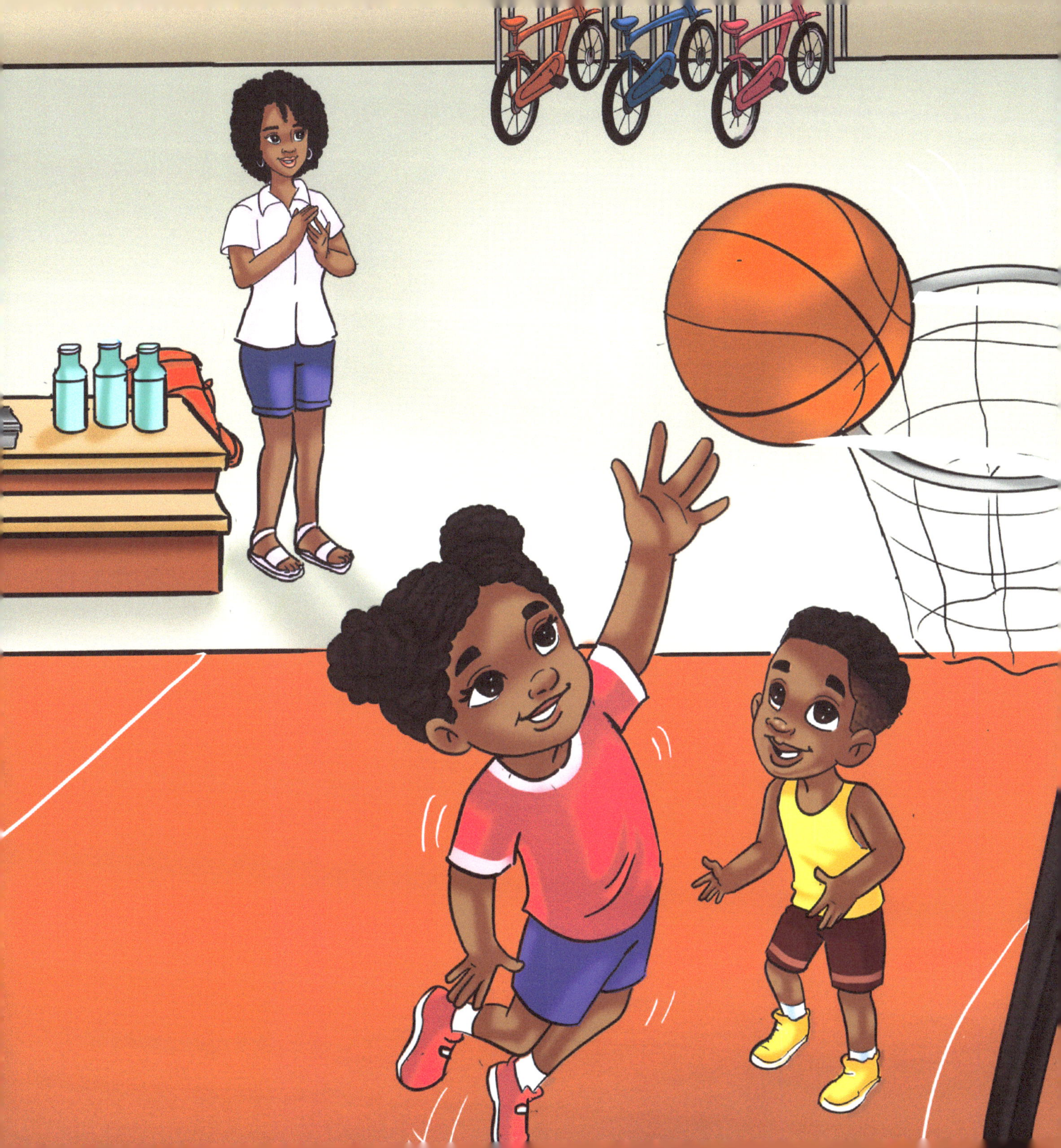

After each player scores a basket,

the other player receives the ball.

Like Layla, Marion shoots and makes his first basket.

Two kids watch the fun that Marion and

Layla are having playing

basketball and want to play as well.

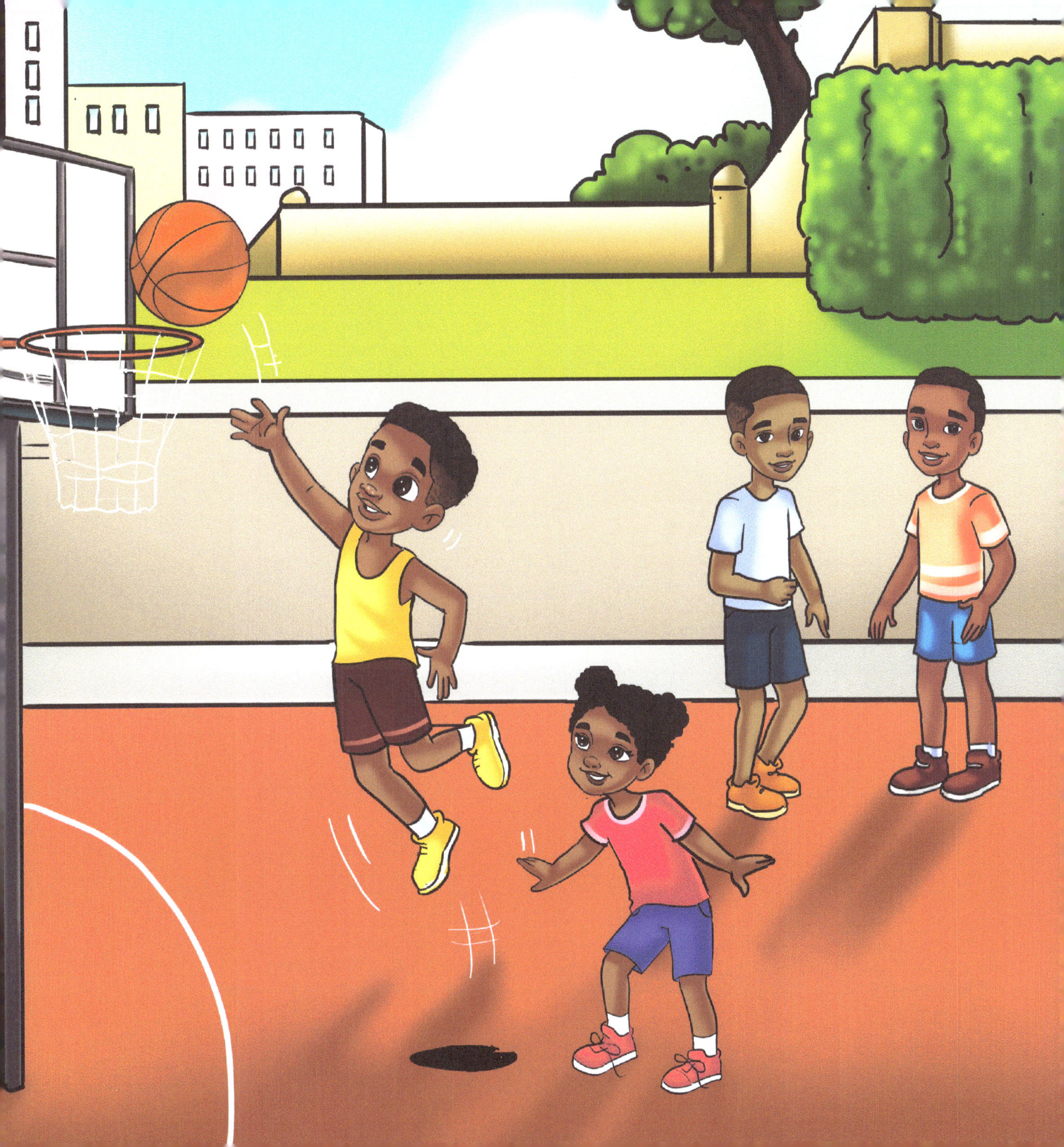

The two kids yell from the courtside to Marion,

"Hey, can we play ball with you two?"

Marion pauses the game with Layla and replies,

"Hey, yes, both of you can play with us." Before starting a new

game, the kids introduce themselves to one another.

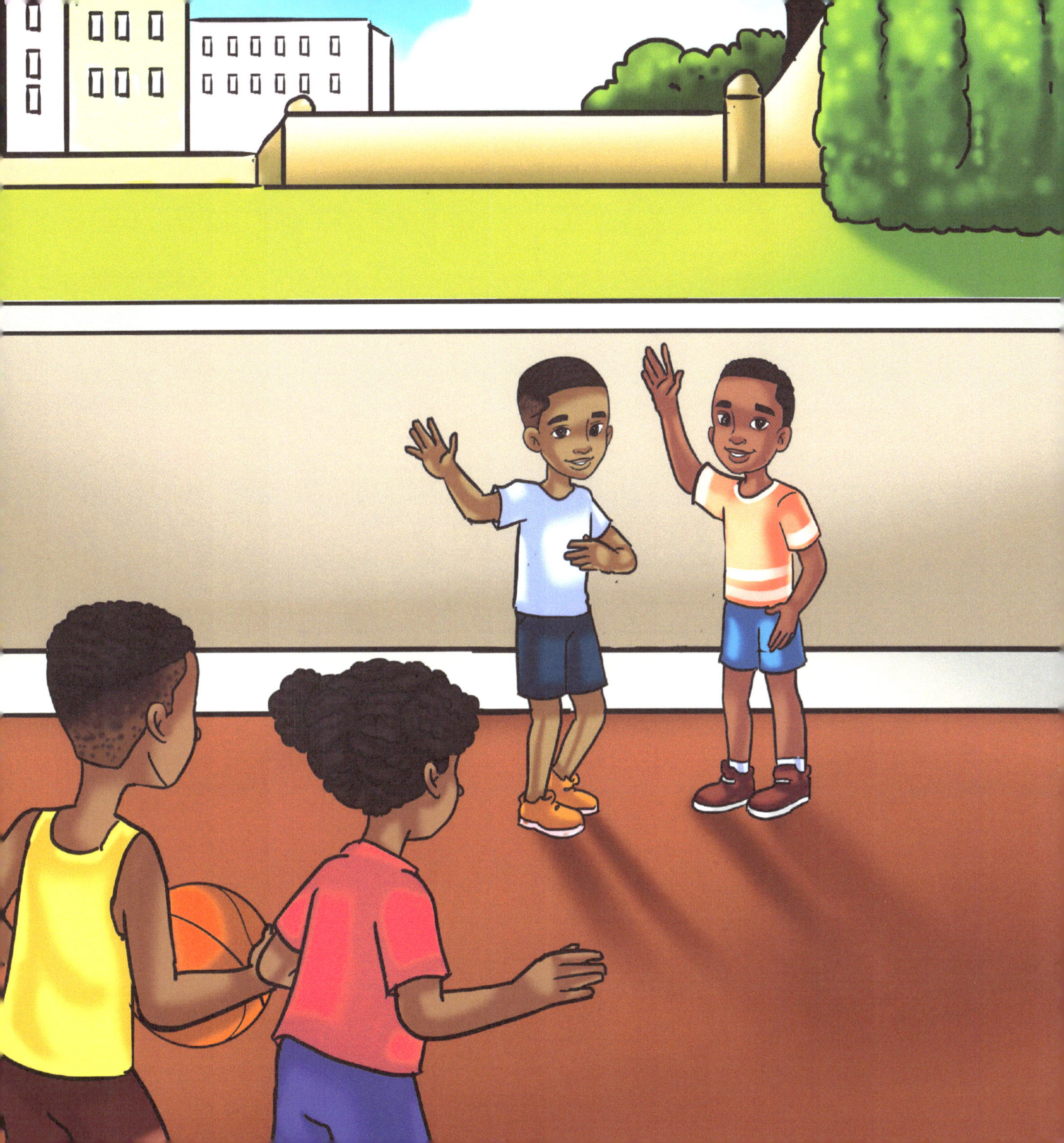

After shaking hands with the

two new players James and Mike, Marion says

"We're excited to play a game together!"

James and Mike replied,

"We're excited too, let's get it!"

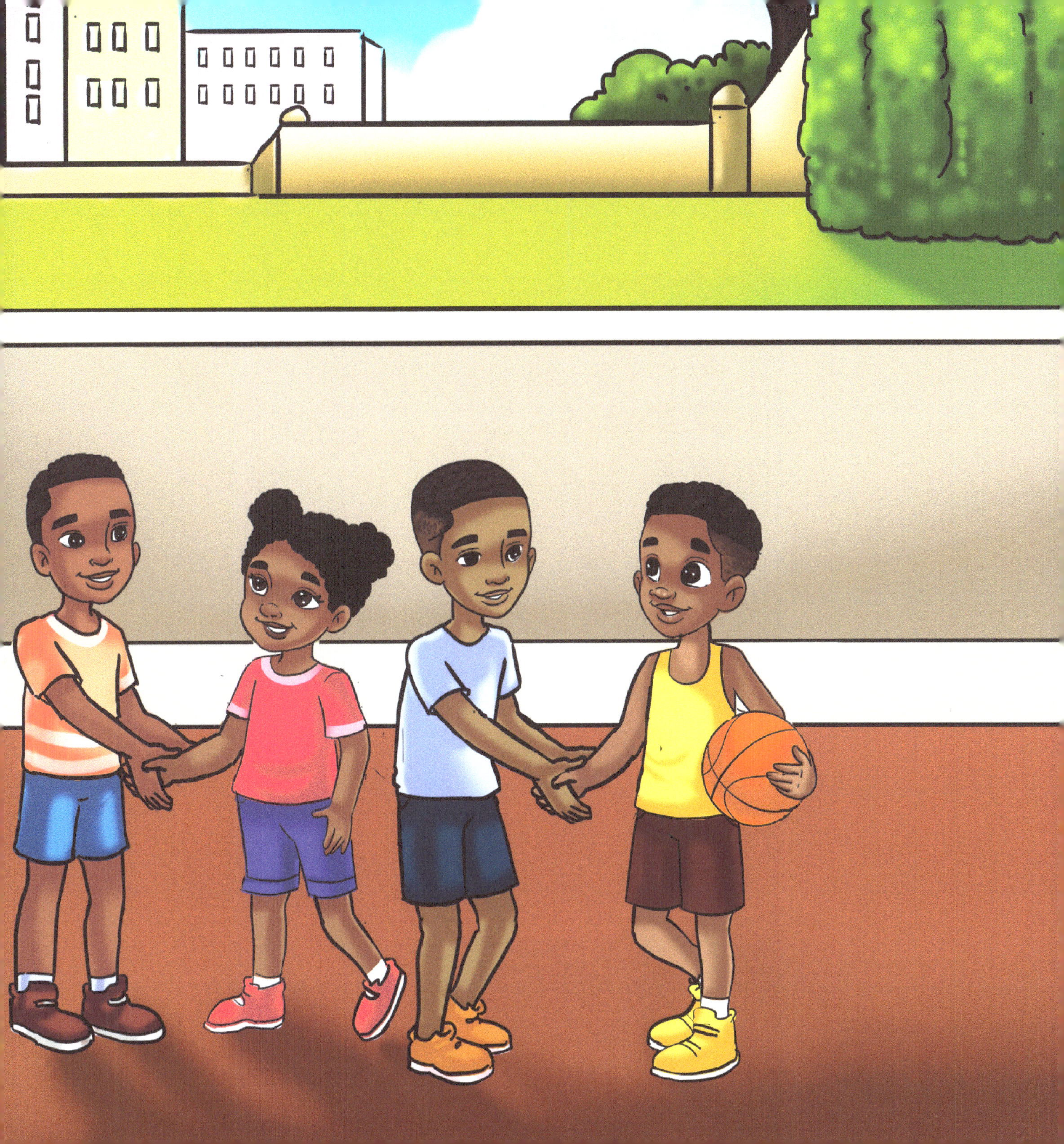

Marion and Layla have the ball first.

After a couple of cool dribbles,

Marion passes the ball to

Layla who puts up a jump shot.

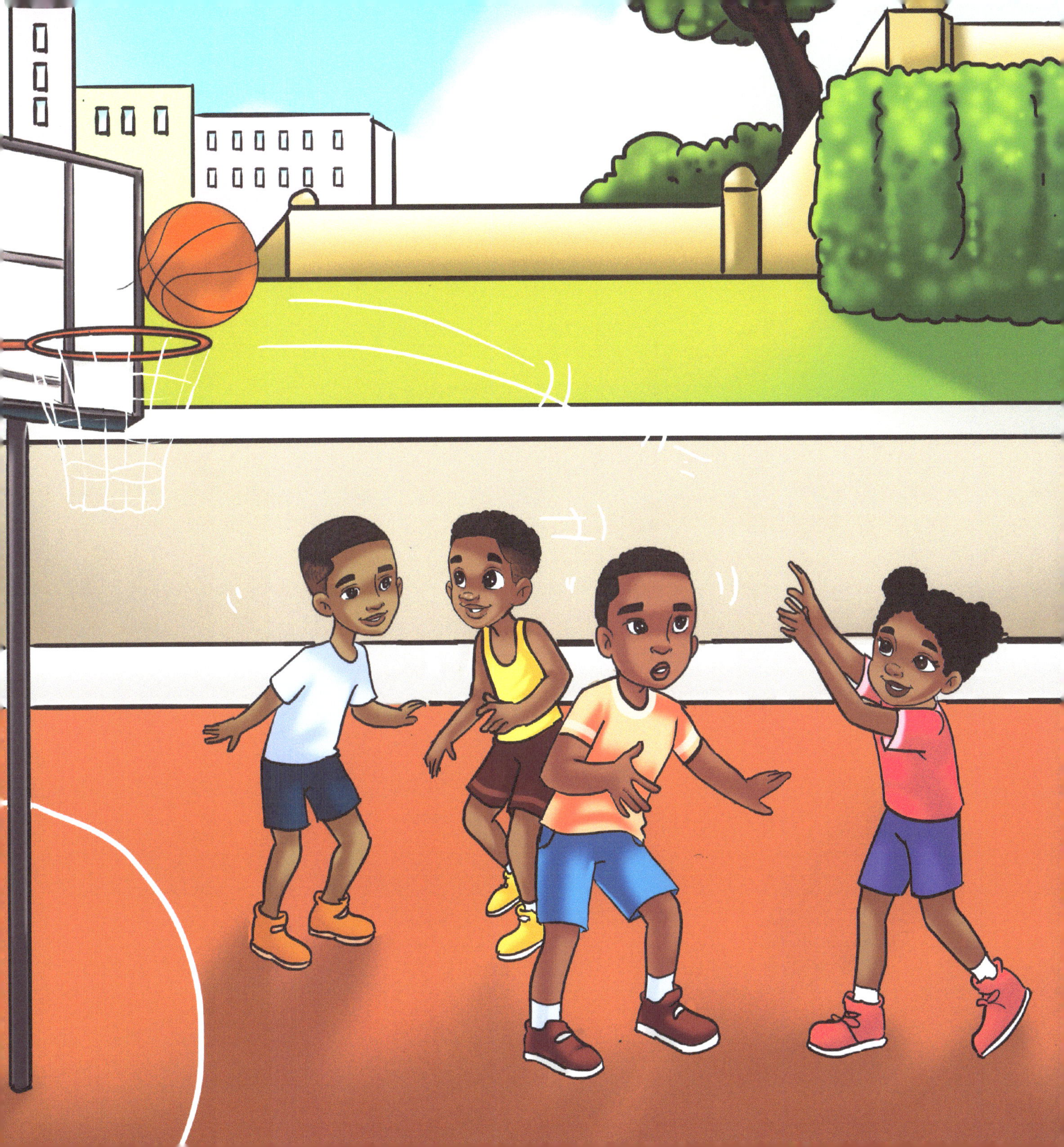

James dribbles the ball. While being guarded by Layla, James passes the ball to Mike. Mike then dribbles and shoots the ball, making the basket. They played a full game and Marion and Layla won with the ending score being 20-18 points.

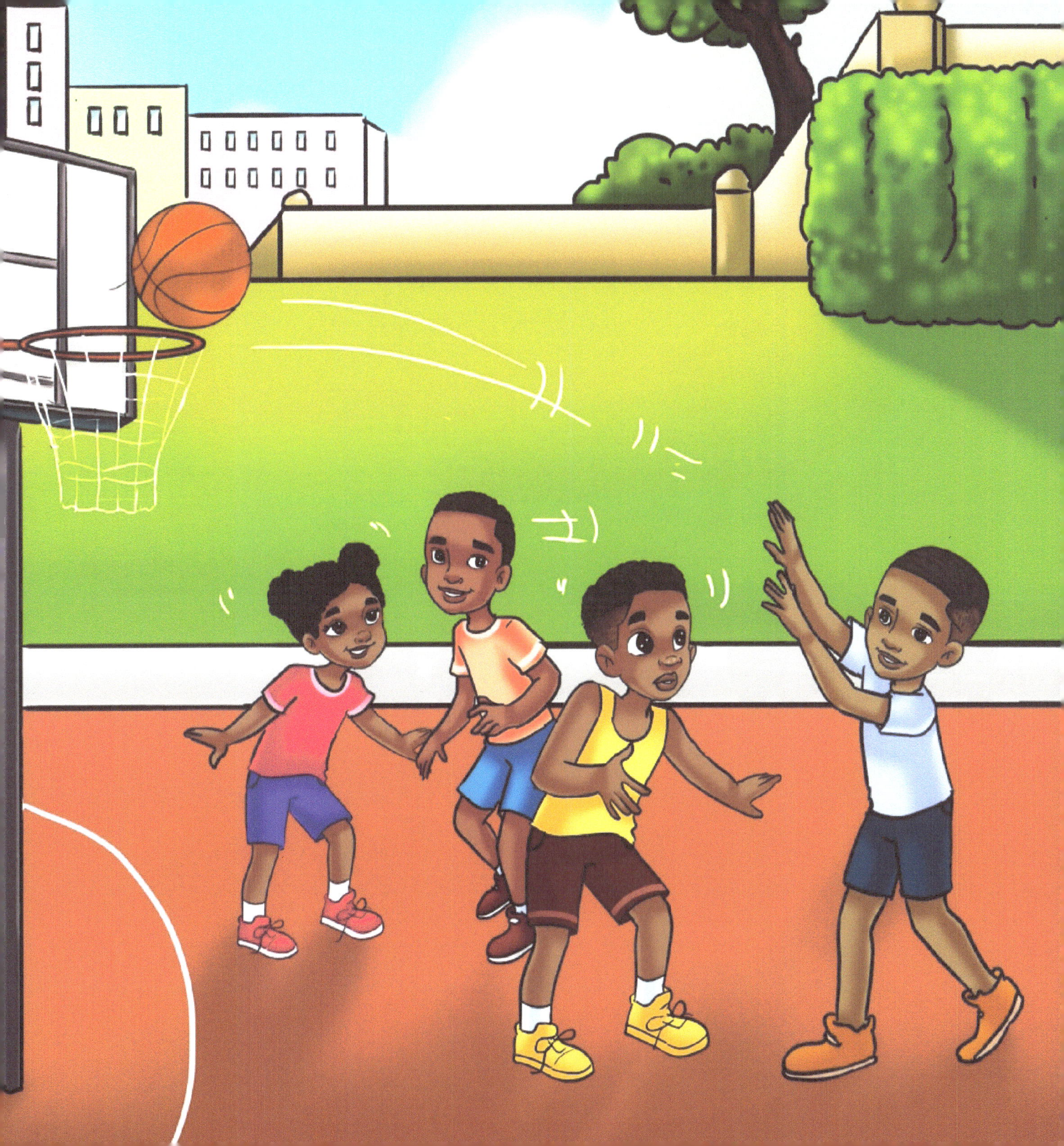

The kids walk over to sit down at the picnic table for a few minutes to catch their breathe before heading over to the carnival.
While sitting down, James and Mike asked Marion and Layla if they were going to the carnival. Marion replied, "Yes, we'll meet you both there shortly."

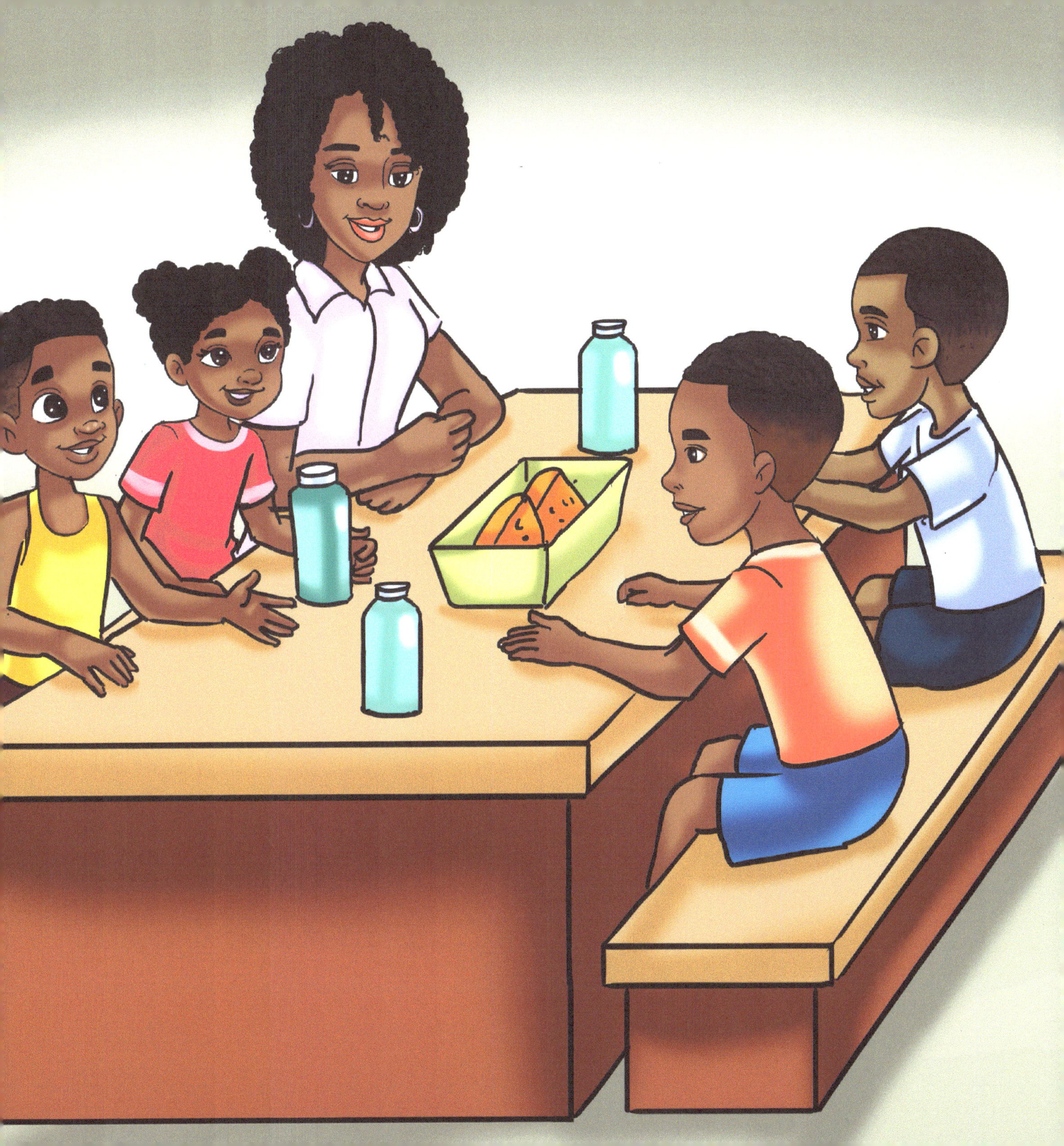

As James and Mike walk away, Marion and Layla stay to talk. Marion said, "I sure wish my dad was here to go to the carnival and ride some of the rides with me."

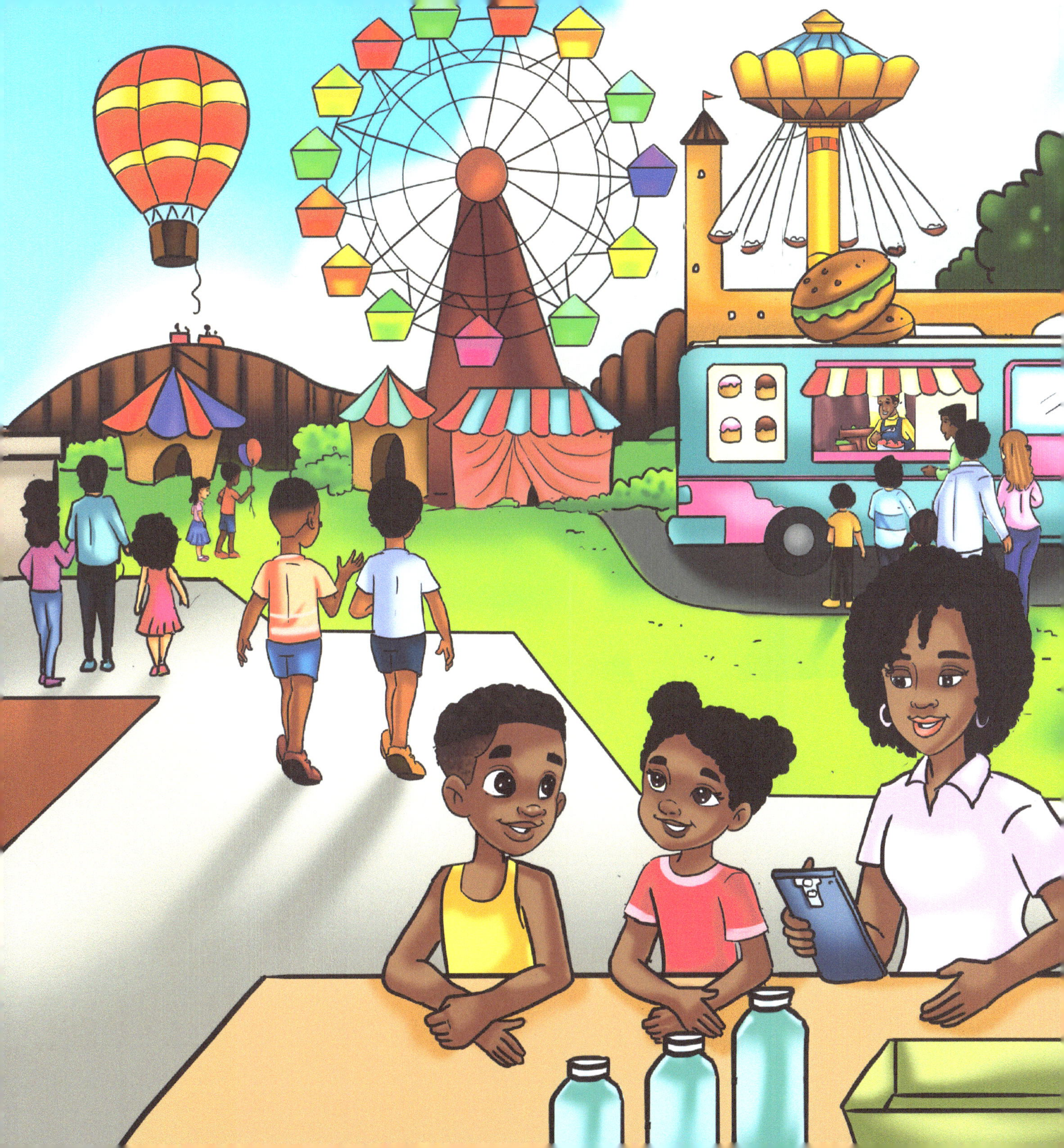

Layla replied, "Yes, I know you must think about that a lot. I wish my mother could watch me play basketball."

"Well, maybe she could join us next time," said Marion.

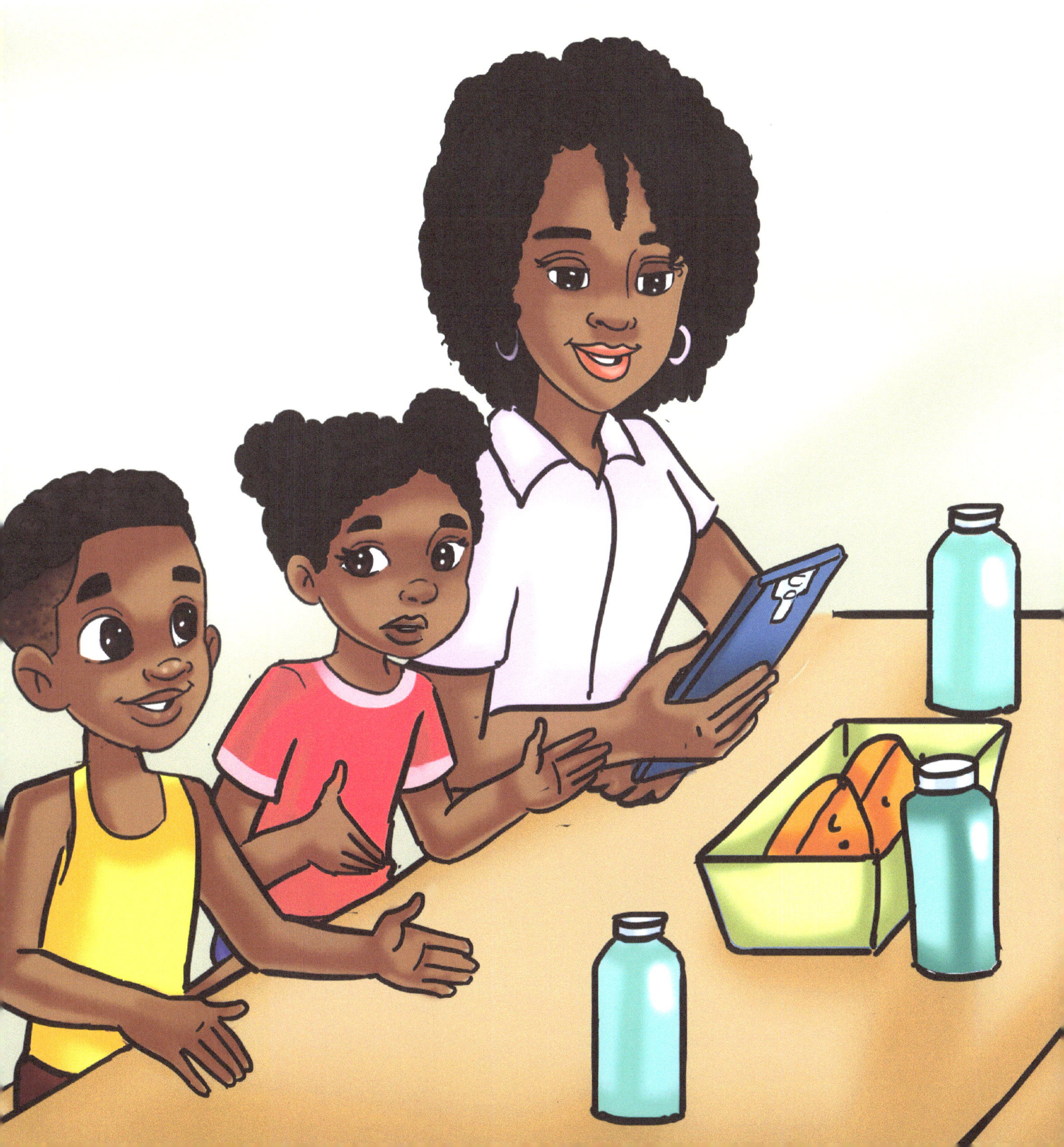

Layla replied, "As much as I would like for my mom to join us, she's unable to. She's very sick and has been in the hospital for quite some time. When it gets hard for me, my dad sits down and have long talks with me so that I would feel better."

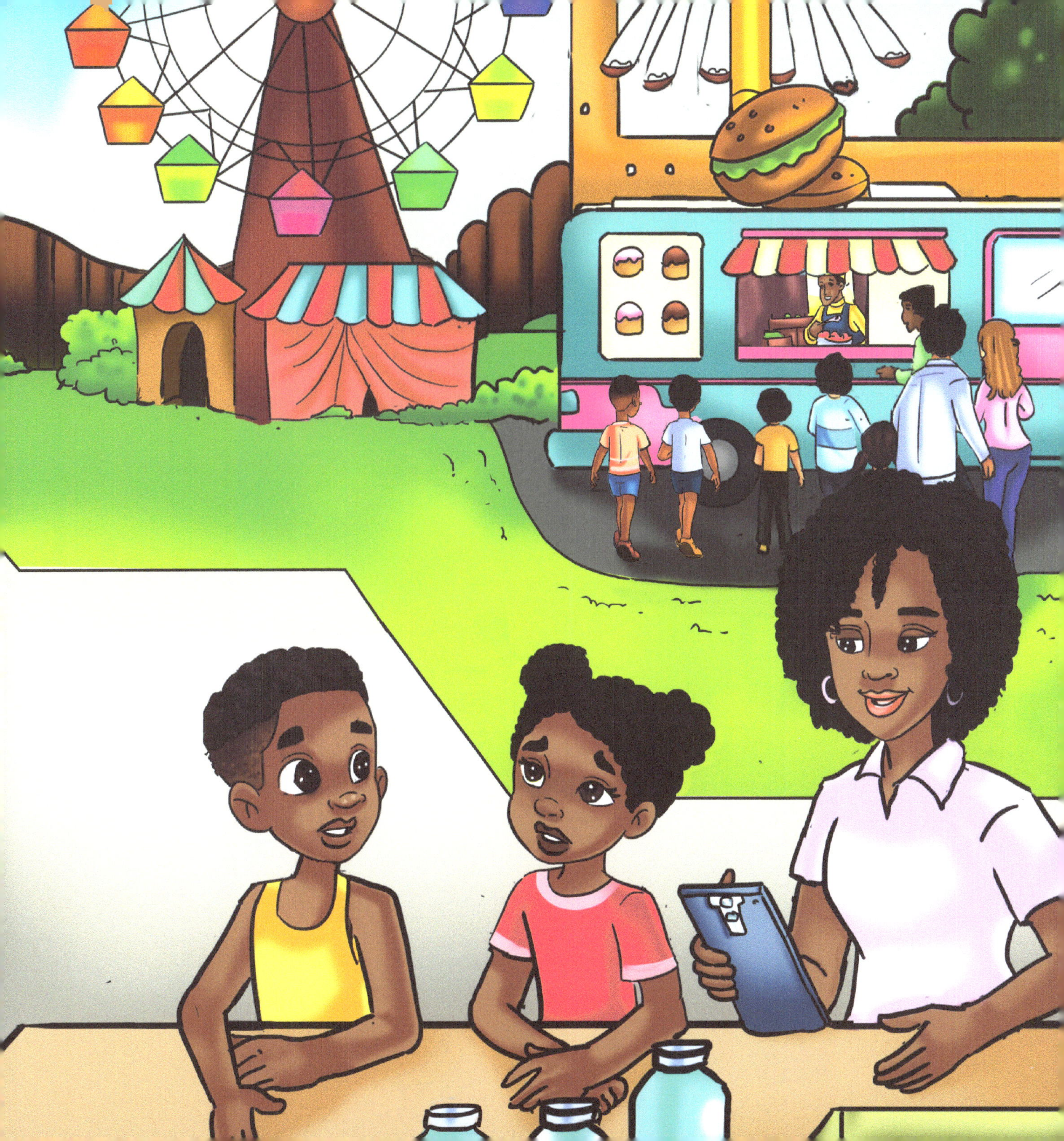

"I know that must be hard for you", Marion responded.

It is hard for me sometimes, but my mom always shows me pictures of my dad. She always tells me how much my dad loved me. We talk about my dad and share great memories of him often."

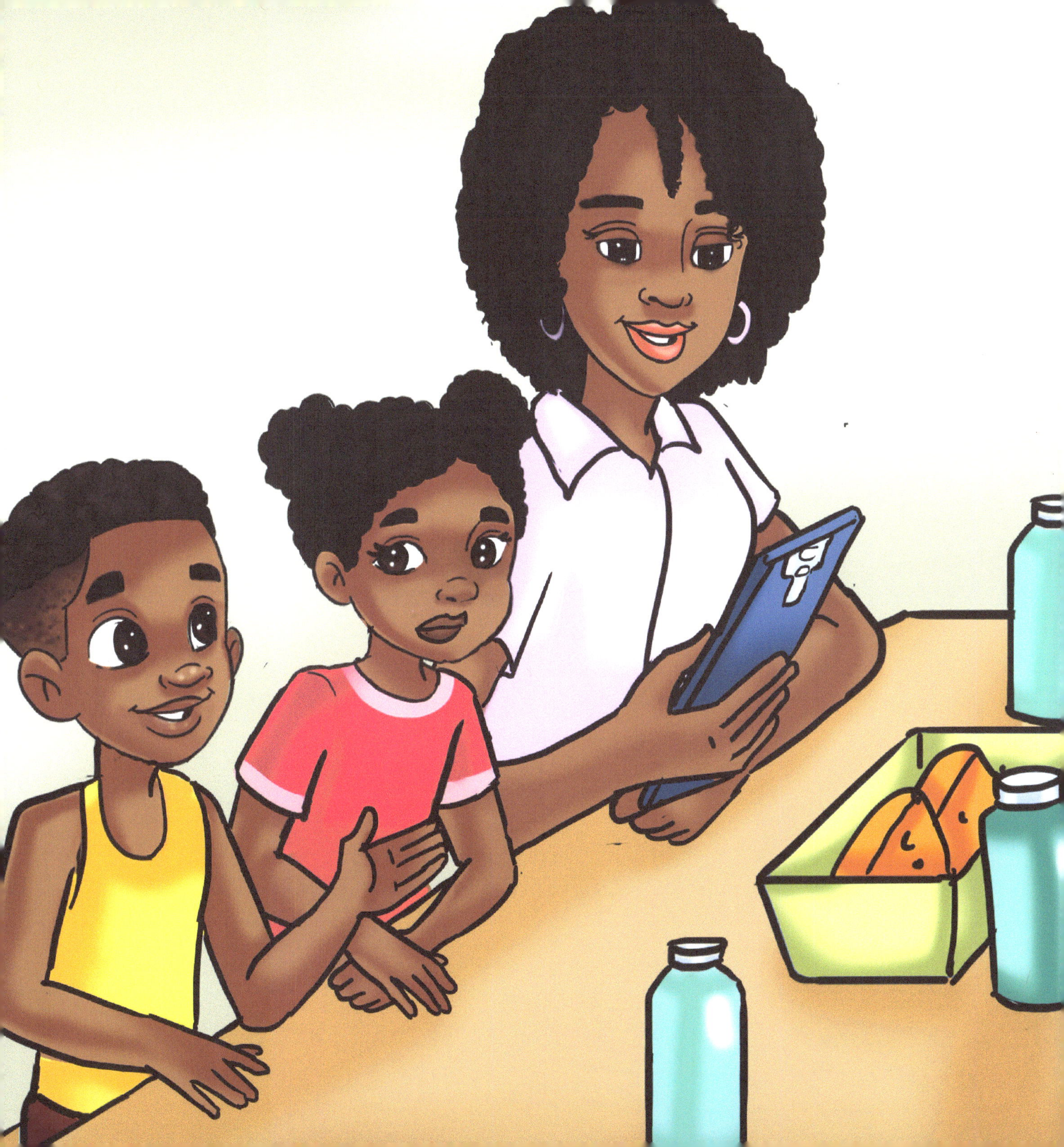

Ms. Myla overheard Marion and Layla discussing how they missed their parents being present. She encourages them by saying, "Always know that although your parents are not here, they love you dearly. Continue to share great memories of your parents and speak about them whenever you'd like to."

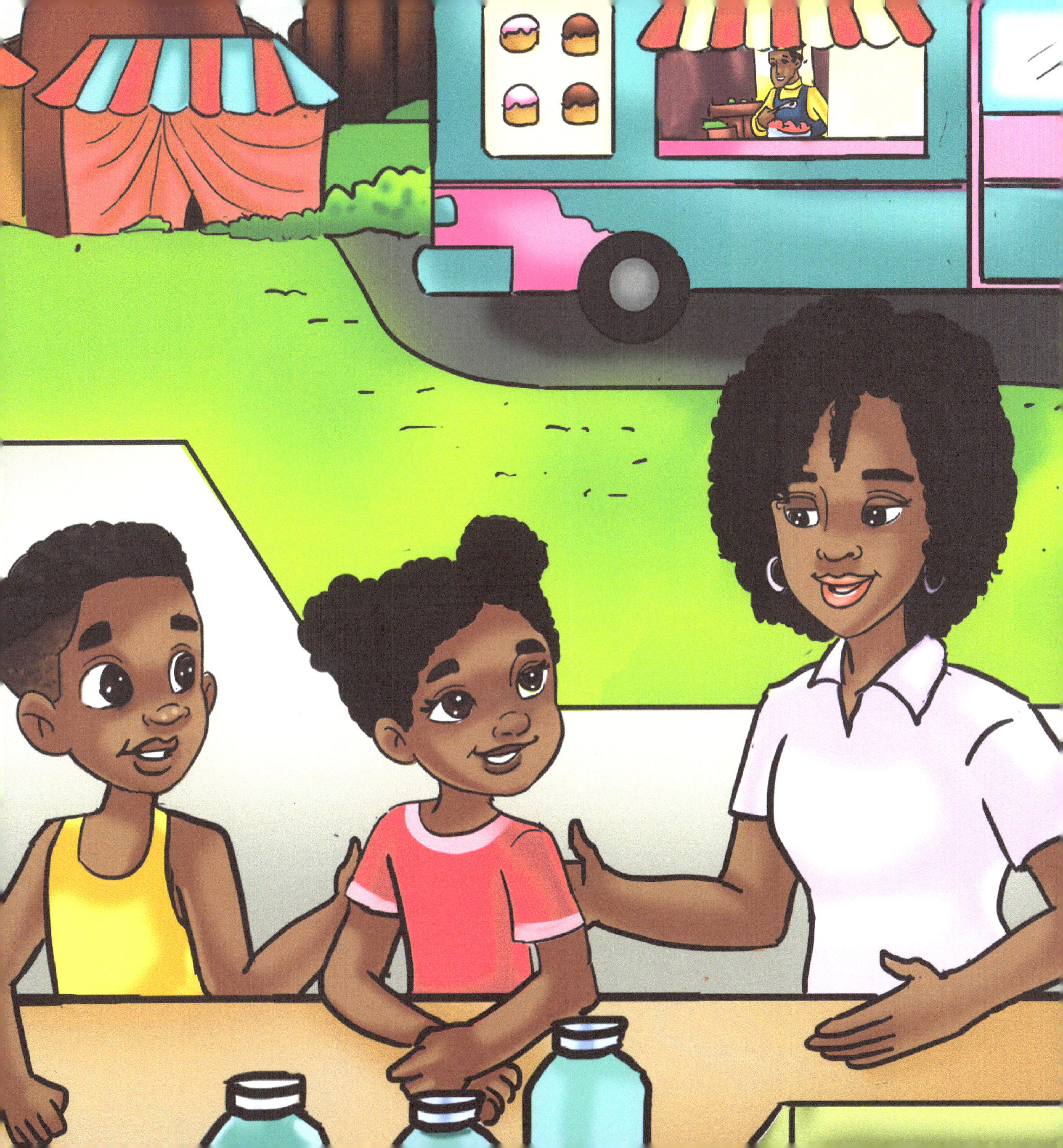

Marion and Layla noticed that James and
Mike have decided to stop at the
food truck ahead of going into the carnival.
So, they, along with Ms. Myla jump in line right behind them.

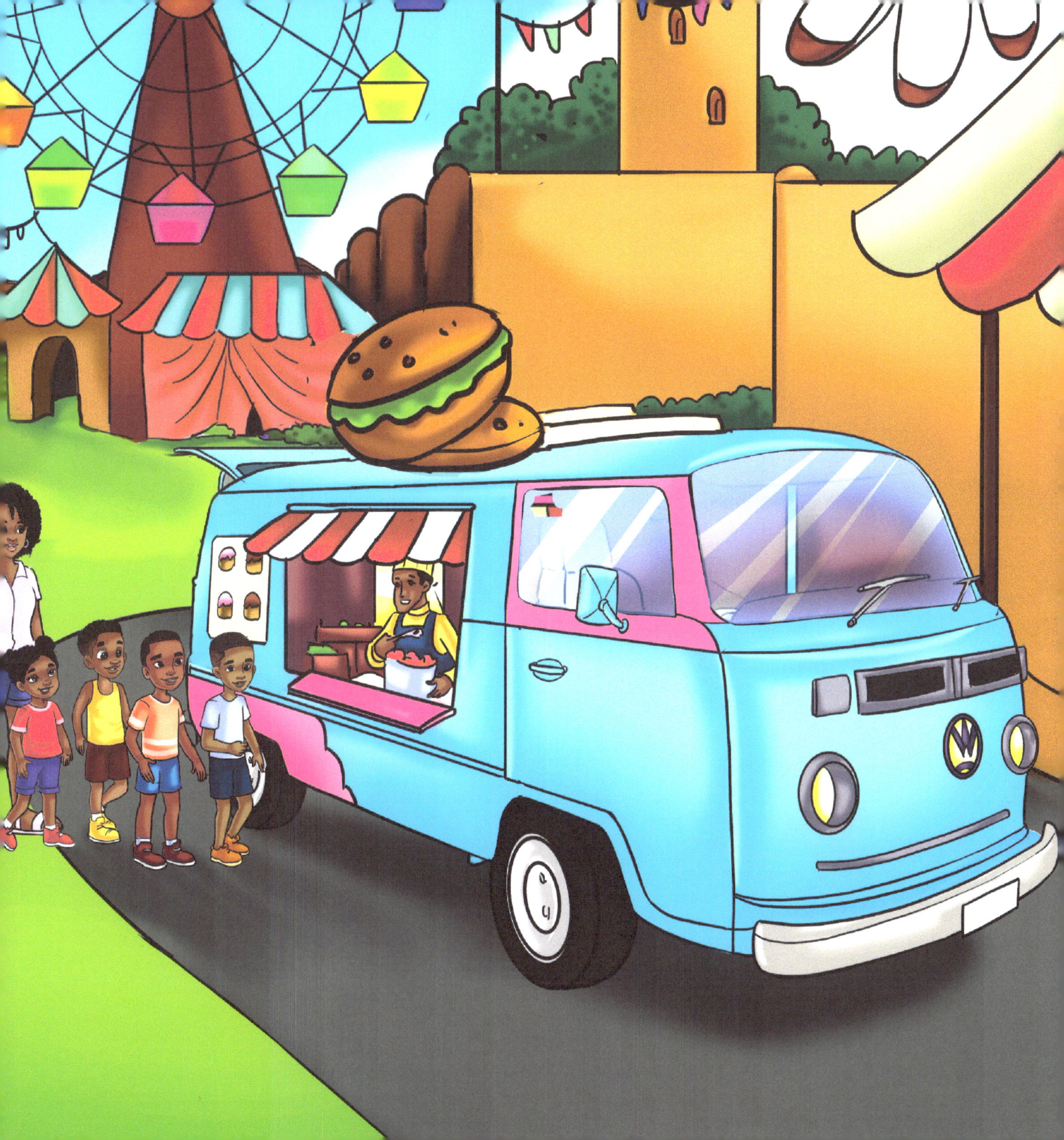

As they sit and eat their food,

the kids began talking about the rides that

they plan to get on.

They decide that their first ride will be the go-carts.

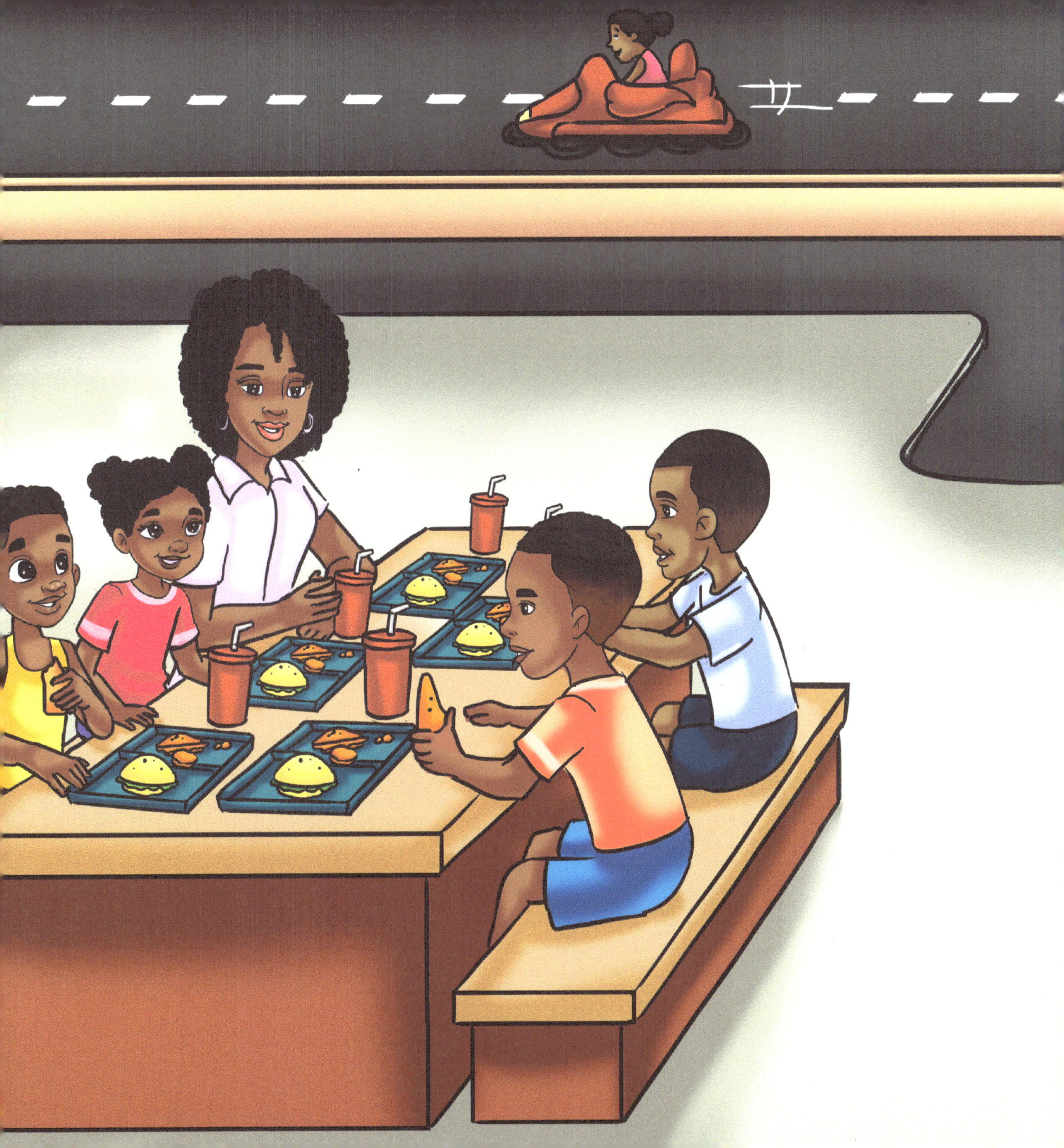

Throughout the rest of the day, Marion, Layla, James, and Mike enjoyed riding several more rides, getting on some multiple times. A day that began with two friends playing ball, ends with making new friends, and creating new memories while learning to cherish other memories.

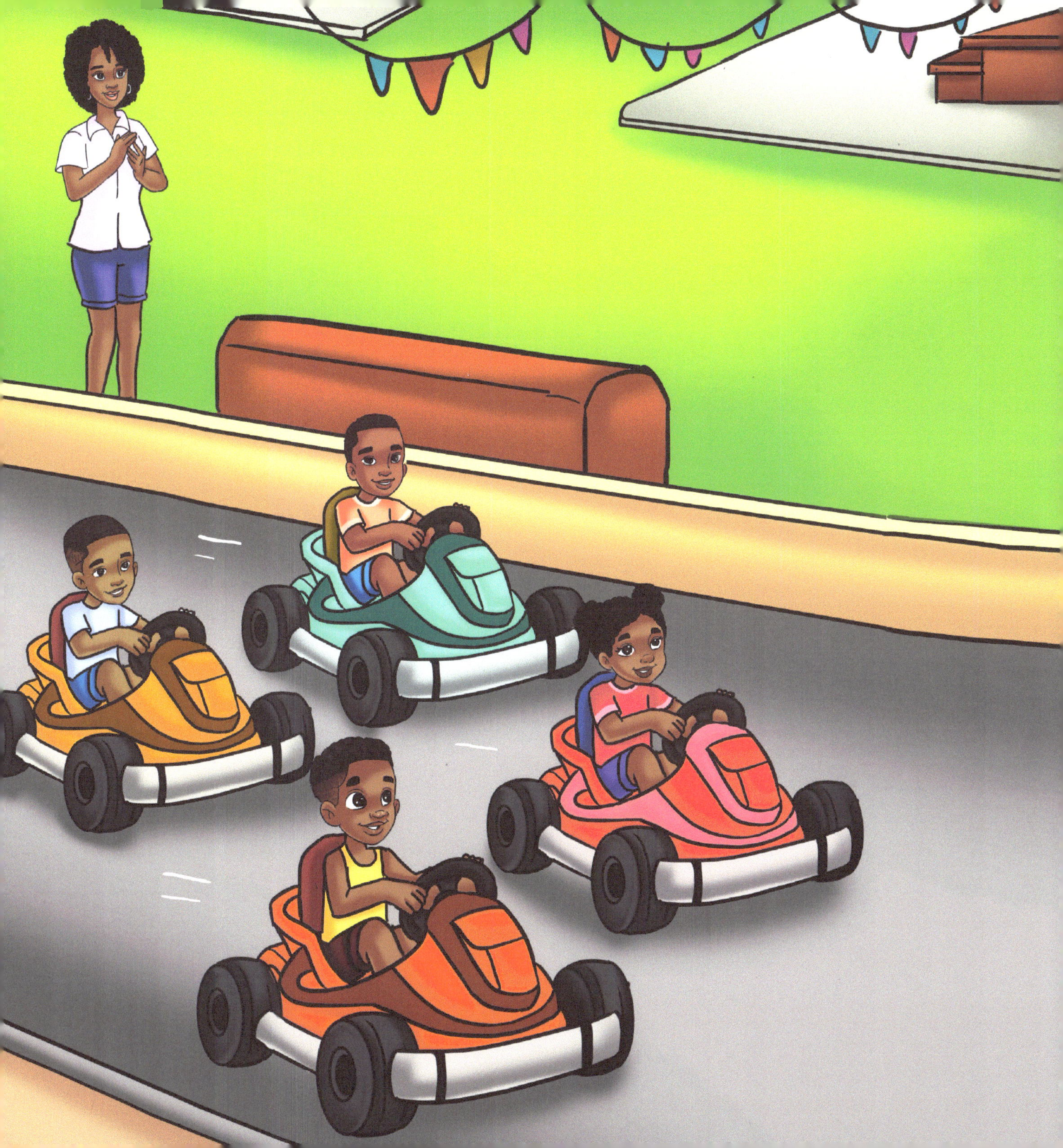

Activity

Draw a picture of you and your parent(s) playing a favorite sport together.

ABOUT THE AUTHOR

Monica Garrett is a retired United States Army Veteran, Certified Grief Coach, and Author who decided to write books to help spread awareness of children dealing with loss and its impacts.

She became a certified grief coach to assist others dealing with grief. Through writing, she hopes to inspire children and others to be strong while on their journey of healing.

>Monica Garrett, M.A.
>Author
>Certified Grief Coach